Anonymous

A Short and Easy Introduction to English Grammar

Explaining those parts of it, which are most necessary and useful, in

speaking or writing: first drawn up for the use of Miss Davies's

boarding-school, Tryon's-Place, Hackney

Anonymous

A Short and Easy Introduction to English Grammar
Explaining those parts of it, which are most necessary and useful, in speaking or writing: first drawn up for the use of Miss Davies's boarding-school, Tryon's-Place, Hackney

ISBN/EAN: 9783337393380

Printed in Europe, USA, Canada, Australia, Japan

Cover: Foto ©Paul-Georg Meister /pixelio.de

More available books at **www.hansebooks.com**

A
SHORT and EASY
INTRODUCTION
TO
ENGLISH GRAMMAR;

Explaining thofe Parts of it, which are moft neceffary and ufeful, in Speaking or Writing.

Firft drawn up for the Ufe of

Mifs DAVIES's BOARDING-SCHOOL,

TRYON's-PLACE, *Hackney;*

And now publifhed, chiefly for the Affiftance of thofe who have the Care of that important Part of Female Education.

LONDON

Printed for J. BUCKLAND, in Paternofter-Row; C. DILLY, in the Poultry; and A. CLEUGH, Ratcliffe-Highway.

M DCC LXXXVI.

A

SHORT and EASY

INTRODUCTION, &c.

Q. WHAT is Grammar?
A. Grammar, in general, is a collection of rules, for speaking or writing any language with propriety.

Q. What is the particular business of English Grammar?
A. To teach the rules which apply to the English language.

Q. What does Grammar treat of?
A. Grammar treats more immediately of Words as connected together in Sentences.

Q. Of what do Words consist?
A. Words consist of Syllables, and Syllables are made up of Letters, one or more.

Of LETTERS.

Q. HOW many Letters are there in Englifh?

A. Twenty-fix: which may be written fmall or large.

Small Letters,

a, b, c, d, e, f, g, h, i, j, k, l, m, n, o, p, q, r, s, t, u, v, w, x, y, z.

Large Letters.

A, B, C, D, E, F, G, H, I, J, K, L, M, N, O, P, Q, R, S, T, U, V, W, X, Y, Z.—The latter are called Capitals.

Q. When are the Capital Letters ufed?

A. At the beginning of fentences, and lines in poetry, to diftinguifh proper names, and other remarkable words.

Q. How are thefe Letters diftinguifhed?

A. Into Vowels and Confonants: fix are Vowels, and all the reft Confonants.

Q. Which are the fix Vowels?

A. A, e, i, o, u, y.

Q. Why

Q. Why are thofe fix Letters called Vowels ?

A. They are called Vowels, becaufe each letter may be diftinctly founded by itfelf.

Q. When are thefe vowels called Diphthongs ?

A. When two of them are united together in one found, as, *ai, oi, ou.*

Q. Why are the other twenty letters called Confonants ?

A. Becaufe they cannot be perfectly founded, unlefs a vowel be joined to them.

Of SYLLABLES.

Q. WHAT is a Syllable ?
A. A Syllable is any number of letters, one of which muft always be a vowel, giving together a diftinct found, and forming a word, or part of a word.

Q. What is Spelling ?

A. Spelling is the art of reading, by firft naming fingly the letters that form a Syllable,

then

then pronouncing that Syllable; and if there
are more than one in a word, joining them
together as you go on, to form that word.
Thus, for example,

Parſimony, *P, a, r,* Par; *ſ, i,* ſi; Parſi;
m, o, mo, Parſimo; *n, y,* ny, Parſimony.

Of WORDS.

Q. HOW many kinds or ſorts of words
are there in the Engliſh language?

A. Nine; commonly called parts of
ſpeech.

Q. What names are given them?

A. Noun, Article, Adjective, Pronoun,
Verb, Adverb, Conjunction, Prepoſition,
and Interjection.

Of NOUNS.

Q. WHAT is a Noun?

A. A Noun is the name of any
thing, as *a Book, a Tree,* &c.

Q. Why

Q. Why is it fometimes called a Subftantive?

A. Becaufe it declares it's own meaning,
and requires no other word to be joined with
it for that purpofe; as *Man, Angel, &c.*

Q. How many kinds of Nouns are there?
A. Two; proper and common.

Q. What is a Noun proper?
A. The name of any individual perfon
or place is a Noun proper; as *Thomas,
London,* &c.

Q. What are Nouns common?
A. Nouns common are fuch names as
exprefs the kinds or forts of things, as *Ani-
mal, Horfe,* &c.

Of the NUMBERS of NOUNS.

Q. HOW many Numbers have Nouns?
A. Two, the fingular and plural.

Q. How are they known or diftinguifhed?
A. The fingular fpeaketh but of one fingle thing, as, *a Book*; the plural, of more
than one, as, *Books.*

B 3   Q. How

Q. How is the Subſtantive ſingular made
plural.

A. By adding *s* or *es* to it, as Book, *Books,*
Box, *Boxes.*

Q. Is it always ſo formed ?

A. No, there are many exceptions to this
rule.

Q. Give me ſome examples?

A. 1. In ſome words ending in *f* the *f* is
changed into a *v*, for the ſound's ſake, as
Leaf in the plural is *Loaves; Calf, Calves.:*
2. In ſome words the plural is formed by
adding *en* or *ren*, as Ox, Ox*en*, Child, Child-
ren. 3. Sometimes by changing *a* to *e*, as
M*a*n, M*e*n ; and ſometimes, 4. By changing
ſeveral letters in the word, as Pen*ny*, P*ence*,
M*ou*ſe, M*i*ce, F*oot*, F*eet*, &c. And, 5. In
ſome few words derived from the Hebrew,
the plural is formed by adding *im* to the ſingular, as Cherub, Cherub*im*.

Q. Have all Nouns a ſingular number ?

A. No ; from the nature of the things
they expreſs, ſome Nouns have no ſingular
number, as *Aſhes, Snuffers, Sciſſors, Wages,* &c.

Q. Have

Q. Have all Nouns a plural Number?

A. No; for the fame reafon fome Nouns have no plural, as the proper names of men and cities, rivers, &c. *Wheat, Pitch, Gold,* and fome others.

Q. Is the plural termination of words always different from the fingular?

A. No: in fome words it is the fame, as *Sheep, Deer.*

Of the CASES of NOUNS.

Q. WHAT do you mean by the Cafes of Nouns?

A. The Cafes of Nouns are their different Endings, to exprefs the different connexions or relations of things one to another.

Q. How many Cafes have Subftantives?

A. In the Englifh language, Nouns have only two different Terminations or Endings for Cafes; namely, the Nominative, and the Genitive or Poffeffive.

Q. What is the Nominative Cafe?

A. The

A. The Nominative Cafe fimply expreffeth the name of the thing, as, *a Boy, a Book.*

Q. What is the Genitive or Poffeffive
Cafe?

A. The Poffeffive Cafe expreffes the thing
to which another thing belongs, or which
may be faid to poffefs or have a property in
that other thing.

Q. How may this Cafe be known?

A. It is formed by adding *s* to the end
of the word, with an apoftrophe or comma
before it, as, The *Boy*'s Book, The *Man*'s
Virtue; that is, The Book of the Boy, the
Virtue of the Man, or the Virtue which
the Man is poffeffed of.

Q. Has the Englifh language no other
method to exprefs the connexions or relations of one thing to another, than by changing the ending of the Subftantive?

A. Yes, it generally ufes for this purpofe
articles or prepofitions, *A, the, of, to, for, O,
from,* or *by,* which partly anfwer to the variation of the end of the Subftantive, in fome
other languages.

OF

Of the GENDER of NOUNS.

Q. WHAT do you mean by the Gender of Nouns?

A. By the Gender of Nouns is meant that form, by which the difference of fex is diftinguifhed.

Q. How many Genders are there?

A. Two; the Mafculine or Male, the Fœminine or Female.

Q. Are all Nouns of thefe Genders?

A. No; fome Nouns are of neither Gender, called therefore Neuter; chiefly applied to the names of things without life.

Q. Do Nouns admit of variation to exprefs the Gender?

A. Yes; to exprefs the Gender fome vary in their ending, as Prince, Prince*fs*; Actor, Ac*trefs*; Hero, Hero*ine*; Executor, Execu*trix*; and fome others.

Q. Do we not fometimes ufe different words to exprefs different Genders?

A. Yes,

A. Yes, in a few inftances ; as Man, *Woman* ; Boy, *Girl* ; Horfe, *Mare* ; Duck, *Drake* ; and fome others.

Q. But how is the diftinction of Genders ufually and moft commonly made?

A. By the words *He*, for the mafculine ; *She*, for the fœminine ; *It*, for the neuter ; that is, when it is neither mafculine nor fœminine ; as, *He* is a *Man*, *She* is a *Woman*, *It* is a *Pen*.

Of ARTICLES.

Q. WHAT is an Article?
A. An Article is a word fet before Nouns, to point them out, and fix the extent of their fignification.

Q. How many Articles are there in the Englifh language?

A. Two ; *A*, which for the found's fake is made *An*, when the word that follows it begins with a vowel ; and *The*.

Q. What

Q. What is the proper ufe of the Article
A or *An?*

A. It ferves to point out one fingle thing
of the kind, without determining what particular thing is meant, as *A* Book, *An* Inkhorn ; that is, any fort of Book, any kind of
Inkhorn.

Q. What is the proper ufe of the Article
The ?

A. The Article *The* determines what particular thing or things are meant, as, This
is *the* Book I loft, the very individual Book :
Thefe are *the* Men I faw yefterday.

Q. Is the Article always placed immediately before the Noun ?

A. No ; fometimes many words come in
between them, as, *A* moft humane and excellent *Man.*

Q. Is not a Noun often ufed without
either of thefe Articles before it ?

A. Yes ; and it is then taken in its wideft
and moft extenfive fenfe ; thus, *Man*, without *A* or *The* before it, fignifies *all Mankind*;
Books, fignify all kinds of Books.

Q. Can

Q. Can you with propriety place the Article *A* before a Noun of the plural number?

A. No; becaufe this Article points out only one fingle thing, A Book, A Pen, we muft not fay, A Books, A Pens.

Q. May you place the Article *The* before a Noun of the plural number?

A. Yes; this Article may be placed before either a fingular or plural Noun, becaufe it determines the particular thing meant, if one; and which they are, if more: as, the Book, or the Books; the Pen, or the Pens.

Of PRONOUNS.

Q. WHAT is a Pronoun?
A. It is a word ufed inftead of a Noun, to avoid a too frequent repetition of the Noun.

Q. How may Pronouns be diftinguifhed?
A. Into perfonal Pronouns, which have the nature of Subftantives, and, as fuch,

4 ftand

ftand by themfelves ; as, *I, Thou, He ;* and
Adjective Pronouns, which have the nature
of Adjectives, and, as fuch, are joined to
Subftantives, as, *Thy, My, Our, Their.*

Q. Why are the firft kind called Perfonal
Pronouns ?

A. Becaufe they mark the perfon or perfons who are the fubject of any difcourfe.

Q. How many perfons may be the fubject of any difcourfe ?

A. Three ; the perfon who fpeaks, the
perfon to whom he fpeaks, or fome other
perfon.

Q. How are thefe three perfons called ?

A. The firft, fecond, and third perfons,
denoted by the words, *I, Thou, He.*

Q. Have they a plural number ?

A. Yes, the fame as Nouns ; becaufe the
Nouns they refer to may be either fingular
or plural.

Q. Have thefe perfonal Pronouns Genders ?

A. Only the third perfon fingular, which

C

has

has the three Genders, Mafculine, *He ;* Fœminine, *She* ; Neuter, *It* ; becaufe this Pronoun refers to a perfon not prefent.

Q. Have thefe perfonal Pronouns Cafes ?
A. Yes, three ; the Nominative, the
Genitive or Poffeffive Cafes, like Nouns ;
and moreover the Objective Cafe, following
Verbs or Prepofitions.

Q. Repeat the Perfonal Pronouns accord-
ing to their perfons and numbers.
A. Singular.   Plural.
I, Thou, He.   We, Ye or You, They.

Q. Repeat the Perfonal Pronouns accord-
ing to their Cafes in each number.
What are the Cafes of the firft perfon ?
A. Singular.   Plural.
Nom. I.   We.
Poff. Mine.   Our or our's.
Obj. Me.   Us.

Q. What are the Cafes of the fecond
perfon ?

A. Singular.

A. Singular.   Plural.
Nom. Thou.   Ye or you.
Poff. Thy or thine. Your's or your.
Obj. Thine.   You.

Q. What are the Cafes of the third per-
fon Mafculine ?
A. Singular.   Plural.
Nom. He.   They.
Poff. His.   Their or their's.
Obj. Him.   Them.

Q. What are the Cafes of the third per-
fon Fœmine ?
A. Singular.   Plural.
Nom. She.   They.
Poff. Her's.   Their's.
Obj. Her.   Them.

Q. What are the Cafes of the third per-
fon Neuter?
A. Singular.   Plural.
Nom. It.   They.
Poff. It's.   Their's.
Obj. It.   Them.

Q. Which are the Adjective Pronouns ?
C 2   A. They

A. They are of feveral kinds, and fome of them thus varied to exprefs Number or Cafes, *My, mine; thy, thine; who, whofe, whom; one, one's; other, other's; this, thefe; that, thofe; felf, felves,* &c.

Q. Are not fome Pronouns without any variation?

A. Yes; as, *Which, what, each, every, whether, either, any, fome, none,* &c.

Q. Are not fome Pronouns diftinguifhed by the name of Relatives?

A. Yes; three principally, *Who, which, that.*

Q. Why are they called Relatives?

A. Becaufe they relate, or more directly refer, to fome Subftantive going before.

Q. What is that Subftantive therefore called?

A. The Antecedent, which fignifies going before.

Q. Are they ufed for any other purpofe?

A. Yes; they are alfo ufed to connect the following part of the fentence with the
foregoing,

foregoing, and fentences one with another : Of which more hereafter.

Of ADJECTIVES.

Q. WHAT is an Adjective?
A. An Adjective is a word added or joined to a Subftantive, and generally going before it, to exprefs it's quality or property, as, A *good* Man, a *bad* Man, a *fine* Houfe, &c.

Q. Do Adjectives admit of any variation?
A. They never vary on account of Number, Gender, or Cafe, but only to form different degrees of Comparifon.

Q. How many degrees of Comparifon are there ?
A. Two ; the Comparative and the Superlative.

Q. What do you mean by the Comparative Degree ?
A. The Comparative Degree is ufed when

the

the quality expreffed by the Adjective is
meant to be fomewhat increafed or diminifhed.

Q. How is it formed?
A. By adding *r* or *er* to the Adjective, as,
Great, great*er*; fmall, fmall*er*.

Q. What is the Superlative Degree?
A. The Superlative Degree is ufed when
the quality expreffed by the Adjective is
meant to be increafed or diminifhed to the
utmoft.

Q. How is it formed?
A. By adding *ft* or *eft* to the end of the
fimple Adjective, as, Great, great*eft*; fmall,
fmall*eft*; wife, wife*ft*.

Q. Is there any other way of forming
thefe Degrees of Comparifon?
A. Yes; the words *more* and *moft* have
the fame effect, as, Wifer, or *more* wife;
wifeft, or *moft* wife.

Q. Are thefe two forms of Comparifon
to be ufed together?
A. No;

A. No; we muſt not ſay more wiſer, moſt wiſeſt, more longer, moſt longeſt, &c.

Q. Are the above invariable rules for forming the Degrees of Compariſon?

A. No; there are many words in this reſpect irregular; that is, their Degrees of Compariſon are not formed by theſe rules, as, *Good, better, beſt; bad, worſe, worſt; many, more, moſt*; and ſome others.

Of VERBS.

Q. WHAT is a Verb?
A. A word ſignifying to do, to ſuffer, or to be.

Q. How are Verbs diſtinguiſhed?
A. Into Verbs Active, Paſſive, and Neuter.

Q. What is a Verb Active?
A. A Verb Active expreſſeth an action, as, To *praiſe*.

Q. What is a Verb Paſſive?
A. A Verb

A. A Verb Paſſive expreſſeth the ſuffering or receiving an action, as, To *be praiſed.*

Q. What general rule is there for diſtinguiſhing Verbs Active and Paſſive ?

A. When the agent takes the lead in a ſentence, the Verb following is Active, as, *William praiſed Mary.* When the object or patient takes the lead, the Verb following is Paſſive, as, *Mary is praiſed by William.*

Q. What is a Verb Neuter ?

A. A Verb Neuter expreſſeth neither action nor paſſion, but merely being, or ſome condition or circumſtance of being, and it's ſenſe is complete without a Noun following it, as, *I am, I reſt.*

Q. Are the ſame Verbs ever uſed both in an Active and Neuter ſenſe ?

A. Yes ; and which of theſe ſenſes they bear in any particular ſentence, may be known by conſidering the nature of the thing which they ſpeak of : As, *Thomas dances,* and *Thomas dances a Minuet* ; in the former of which the Verb is Neuter, in the latter Active.

4

Q. What

Q. What are the chief things to be con-
fidered in a Verb ?

A. It's Perfon, Number, Time, and
Mode.

Q. What do you mean by the Perfon of
a Verb?

A. It's agreement with one or other of
the perfonal Pronouns, *I, Thou, He,* in either
the fingular or plural number.

Q. Does it not fometimes vary it's ending, to exprefs or agree with different Perfons or Numbers?

A. Yes, as, I love, thou love*ſt,* he lov-
eth, &c.

Q. With what does the Verb agree in
Number ?

A. It agrees in Number with the number
of the Noun or Pronoun going before it, as,
The *Man hateth* me, They *love* me.

Of the MODES of VERBS.

Q. WHAT are the Modes of Verbs?
A. The Modes of Verbs are the Methods of ufing the Verb to reprefent the *manner* of the Being, Action, or Paffion, exprefled by that Verb.

Q. How many Modes of Verbs are there in Englifh?
A. Four: the Indicative, the Imperative, the Subjunctive, and the Infinitive.

Q. What is the Indicative Mode?
A. The Indicative Mode fimply declareth fomewhat, or afketh a queftion, as, *I read. Readeft thou?*

Q. What is the Imperative Mode?
A. The Imperative Mode commandeth, entreateth, or permitteth, as, *Read thou*, or, *let him read.*

Q. What is the Subjunctive Mode?
A. The Subjunctive Mode expreffeth the
Action

Action or Being as poffible or impoffible, fit or unfit, as doubtful or uncertain.

Q. Why is it called the Subjunctive Mode?

A. Becaufe for the moft part it depends on fome other Verb, or has a Conjunction before it, as, I *may love*, *If I love*, I *wifh* I *could* love.

Q. What is the Infinitive Mode?

A. The Infinitive Mode expreffeth the Verb without any limitation of perfon or number, and generally with the Præpofition, *to*, before it, as, *To love*.

Q. What is a Participle?

A. A Participle is part of a Verb, which fometimes partakes of the nature of an Adjective.

Q. How many Participles has a Verb?

A. Two; one of the Prefent Tenfe, ending in *ing*, as lov*ing*; and one of the Præterite Tenfe, called alfo the Paffive Participle, ending in *ed*; or in *d* only, when the Verb ends in *e*, as, turn, turn*ed*; love, love*d*.

Of

Of the TENSES of VERBS.

Q. WHAT do you mean by the Tenſes of Verbs ?

A. The manner of uſing the Verb to expreſs the different times in which any thing is repreſented as exiſting, acting, or acted upon.

Q. What is the firſt natural Diviſion of Time ?

A. Into Paſt, Preſent, and Future.

Q. What follows from hence ?

A. That there are three Tenſes, which may be called Primary or Indefinite Tenſes.

Q. Which are they ?

A. The Preſent, the Præterite or Paſt, and Future.

Q. Have we no occaſion to ſpeak of Time, but as Preſent, Paſt, and Future ?

A. Yes ; we have often occaſion to ſpeak of Time with ſome further particular diftinction

tinction or limitation, that is, as paſſing or imperfect, or as finiſhed and perfect.

Q. What follows from this?

A. Two Tenſes, to mark theſe particular diſtinctions in each of the primary Tenſes, which may be called Definitive Tenſes.

Q. Which are they?

A. Preſent imperfect,　I am loving.
Preſent perfect,　　I have loved.

Paſt imperfect, or,⎫
Præter imperfect,　⎬I was loving.

Paſt perfect, or　⎫
Præter perfect,　⎬I had loved.

Future imperfect,　I ſhall be loving.
Future perfect,　　I ſhall have loved.

Q. How are theſe different times expreſſed?

A. The Verb ſometimes varies its termination to expreſs different times; but very often uſes alſo the aſſiſtance of other words for this purpoſe.

Q. What are theſe words called?

A. Auxiliaries,

A. Auxiliaries, or Helpers, put before the Verb as figns of the Tenfe; as, I *do* love, I *am* loved, &c.

Q. Which are the principal of thefe?
A. *Have, be, do, let, may, can, fhall, will, muft.*

Q. Are not fome of thefe Verbs?
A. Yes; fome of them are proper Verbs, but fometimes are ufed only as figns of the Perfon, Numbers, Tenfes, and Mode of other Verbs.

Q. How are they varied according to Perfon, Number, Time, and Mode? and firft, how is *Have* varied?

INDICATIVE MODE.

Prefent Tenfe.

Perfon.	Singular.	Plural.
1.	I have.	We have.
2.	Thou haft.	Ye have.
3.	He hath or has.	They have.

Præterite

Præterite Tenſe.

Perſon.	Singular.	Plural.
1.	I had.	We had.
2.	Thou hadſt.	Ye had.
3.	He had.	They had.

Future Tenſe.

Perſon.	Singular.	Plural.
1.	I ſhall or will have.	We ſhall or will have.
2.	Thou ſhalt or wilt have.	Ye ſhall or will have.
3.	He ſhall or will have.	They ſhall or will have.

IMPERATIVE MODE.

Perſon.	Singular.	Plural.
1.	Let me have.	Let us have.
2.	Have thou, or do thou have.	Have ye, or do ye have.
3.	Let him have.	Let them have.

SUB-

SUBJUNCTIVE MODE.

Prefent Tenfe.

Perfon.	Singular.	Plural.
1.	I have.	We have.
2.	Thou have.	Ye have.
3.	He have.	They have.

INFINITIVE MODE.

Prefent, To have : Paft, To have had.

Participle.

Prefent, Having : Perfect, Had : Paft, Having had.

Q. How is the Auxiliary *Be* varied ?

INDICATIVE MODE.

Prefent Tenfe.

Perfon.	Singular.	Plural.
1.	I am.	We are.
2.	Thou art.	Ye are.
3.	He is.	They are.

Præterite

Præterite Tenſe.

Perſon.	Singular.	Plural.
1.	I was.	We were.
2.	Thou waſt.	Ye were.
3.	He was.	They were.

Future Tenſe.

Perſon.	Singular.	Plural.
1.	I ſhall or will be.	We ſhall or will be.
2.	Thou ſhalt or wilt be.	Ye ſhall or will be.
3.	He ſhall or will be.	They ſhall or will be.

IMPERATIVE MODE.

Perſon.	Singular.	Plural.
1.	Let me be.	Let us be.
2.	Be or be thou.	Be or be ye.
3.	Let him be.	Let them be.

D 3,   SUB-

SUBJUNCTIVE MODE.

Prefent Tenfe.

Perfon.	Singular.	Plural.
1.	If I be.	If we be.
2.	If thou beeft.	If ye be.
3.	If he be.	If they be.

Præterite Tenfe.

Perfon.	Singular.	Plural.
1.	If I were.	If we were.
2.	If thou wert.	If ye were.
3.	If he were.	If they were.

INFINITIVE MODE.

Prefent, To be: Paft, To have been.

Participle.

Prefent, Being: Perfect, Been: Paft,
Having been.

Q. How

[31]

Q. How is the Auxiliary *Do* varied ?

INDICATIVE MODE.

Prefent Tenfe.

Perfon.	Singular.	Plural.
1.	I do.	We do.
2.	Thou doeft or doft.	Ye do.
3.	He doeth or does.	They do.

Præterite Tenfe.

Perfon.	Singular.	Plural.
1.	I did.	We did.
2.	Thou didft.	Ye did.
3.	He did.	They did.

Participle.

Prefent, Doing : Præterite, Done.

Q. What Variations has the Auxiliary *May* ?
A. *May, mayeft ; might, mighteft.*

Q. What

Q. What are the Variations of the Auxiliary *Can* ?

A. *Can, canſt ; could, couldeſt.*

Q. How is the Auxiliary *Shall* varied ?

A. *Shall, ſhalt ; ſhould, ſhouldeſt.*

Q. What are the Variations of the Auxiliary *Will* ?

A. *Will, wilt ; would, wouldeſt.*

Q. Have *Let* and *Muſt* any Variations ?

A. *Muſt* varies not ; nor has *Let* any variation as an Auxiliary.

Q. How is a Verb Active, with its Auxiliaries, varied through it's Perſons, Numbers, Modes, and Primary or Indefinite Times or Tenſes ?

INDICATIVE MODE.
Preſent Tenſe.

Perſon.	Singular.	Plural.
1.	I love or do love.	We love.
2.	Thou loveſt or doſt love.	} Ye love.
3.	He loveth or doth love.	They love or do love.

Paſt

Paſt Time, or Præterite Tenſe.

Perſon.	Singular.	Plural.
1.	I loved or have loved.	We loved or have loved.
2.	Thou lovedſt or haſt loved.	Ye loved or have loved.
3.	He loved or hath loved.	They loved or have loved.

Future Tenſe.

Perſon.	Singular.	Plural.
1.	I ſhall or will love.	We ſhall or will love.
2.	Thou ſhalt or wilt love.	Ye ſhall or will love.
3.	He ſhall or will love.	They ſhall or will love.

IMPERATIVE MODE.

Perſon.	Singular.	Plural.
1.	Let me love.	Let us love.
2.	Love thou, or do thou love.	Love ye, or do ye love.
3.	Let him love.	Let them love.

SUB-

SUBJUNCTIVE MODE.

Prefent Tenfe.

Perfon.	Singular.	Plural.
1.	I may or can love.	We may or can love.
2.	Thou mayeft or canft love.	Ye may or can love.
3.	He may or can love.	They may or can love.

Paft Time, or Præterite Tenfe.

Perfon.	Singular.	Plural.
1.	I might love.	We might love.
2.	Thou mighteft love.	Ye might love.
3.	He might love.	They might love.

And,

I could, or fhould, or would.
Thou couldeft, fhouldeft, or wouldeft love
or have loved.

Future

Future Tenfe.

Perfon.	Singular.	Plural.
1.	I fhall have loved.	We fhall have loved.
2.	Thou fhalt have loved.	Ye fhall have loved.
3.	He fhall have loved.	They fhall have loved.

Q. What may be particularly obferved of the Tenfes of this Mode?

A. That in this Subjunctive Mode the precife Time of the Verb is very much determined by the nature and drift of the fentence.

Q. How comes this to pafs?

A. Becaufe the Verb and Auxiliary of the Prefent Tenfe often carry with them a Future Senfe, and the Auxiliaries *Should* and *Would* are ufed to exprefs the Prefent and Future, as well as the Paft Time.

Prefent Tenfe,   To love.
Paft,   To have loved.

Participle.

Prefent,   Loving.
Perfect,   Loved.
Paft,   Having loved.

Q. Why have you not the Variations of the Definite Tenfes fet down here?

A. Becaufe they change not the Termination of the Verb, but confift only of the proper Variations of the Auxiliary, joined to the Prefent or Perfect Participle, which have been already given.

Q. How is a Verb Paffive varied?

A. The Verb Paffive does not vary it's Termination at all, which is the fame as the Perfect Participle.

Q. How then are the Perfons, Numbers, Times, and Modes expreffed?

3   A. By

A. By the Auxiliary *Be,* through all it's Variations, joined to it ; as, I *am* loved, I *was* loved, I *have been* loved, If I *were* loved, &c.

Q. How is the Verb Neuter varied?
A. In general like the Active, though, in many inftances, it admits the Paffive form, ftill retaining it's Neuter fignification.

Of IRREGULAR VERBS.

Q. DO you remember how we faid the Paft Time Active and the Participle Perfect, or Paffive, are formed?
A. Yes ; by adding to the Verb *ed,* or *d* only, when the Verb ends in *e,* as, Turn, turn*ed* ; love, lov*ed*.

Q. What are Irregular Verbs?
A. Thofe which vary from this rule in forming the Præterite Tenfe, or Perfect Participle, are called Irregular. *For a table of Irregular Verbs, fee the Appendix.*

E   Of

Q. WHAT are Adverbs?

A. Adverbs are words added chiefly to Verbs or Adjectives, to mark some circumstance or manner of an action, as, *wifely*, that is, in a *wife manner*; *now*, that is, *at this time*.

Q. How many kinds of Adverbs are there?

A. Adverbs are divided into many kinds, but the principal of them are Adverbs of place, as, *Here, There;* those of time, as, *often, sometimes;* and those of quality or manner, as, *wifely, happily,* &c.

Q. How do many of them end in the English language?

A. Very many of them end in *ly,* as, Happi*ly,* Wife*ly,* &c. and are derived from Adjectives, by adding this syllable to them, as, Wife, wife*ly;* happy, happi*ly.*

Q. Do Adverbs admit of any variation?

A. No,

A. No, except some few, which admit of degrees of comparison, as, *Often, oftener, oftenest; well, better, best; soon, sooner, soonest.*

Of CONJUNCTIONS.

Q. WHAT is the use of Conjunctions?

A. To join words and sentences together, as, You *and* I went out, *but* it rained *and* we returned.

Q. How many sorts or kinds of Conjunctions are there?

A. Principally two; copulative and disjunctive.

Q. What is the use of the Copulative Conjunction?

A. The use of the Copulative Conjunction is to connect or to continue the sentence.

Q. What is the use of the Disjunctive Conjunction?

E 2

A. The

A. The use of the Disjunctive is likewise to connect and continue the sentence, but to mark at the same time opposition or distinction in the sense of the things spoken of, as, *or*, *but*, *than*, *although*, *unless*, &c. It is one *or* other ; This is a good Book, *but* not perfect, &c.

Of PRÆPOSITIONS.

Q. WHAT is a Præposition ?

A. A Præposition is a word put before other words, to shew the relation of words to each other ; such as, *Of*, *from*, *with*, *to*. He bought it *with* money ; He went *from* London *to* Hackney.

Of INTERJECTIONS.

Q. WHAT is an Interjection ?

A. An Interjection is a word introduced into a sentence, denoting some sudden or peculiar emotion or passion of the mind, as, *Ah!* *Oh!* *Alas!* &c.

OF

Of SENTENCES.

Q. WHAT is a Sentence?
A. A Sentence is a certain number of words connected together, and so constructed as to make a complete sense.

Q. On what does the just form and construction of such words depend?
A. Chiefly on their concord or agreement, and on their government and position.

Q. What do you mean by the Concord or Agreement of Words?
A. One word is said to agree with another, when it is required to be in like Case, Number, Gender, or Person.

Q. What do you mean by the Government of Words?
A. One word governs another, when it causeth that other to be in some Case or Mode.

E 3   Q. What

Q. What is meant by the Pofition of Words?

A. By the Pofition of Words is meant the due and proper order of them in a Sentence, fo as to exprefs the fenfe intended.

Q. How may Sentences be divided?
A. Into Simple and Compound.

Q. What is a Simple Sentence?
A. A Simple Sentence has in it but one agent or fubject, and one Verb, or two with the latter in the Infinitive Mode, and may alfo include one object; as, Mary improves her Time; and, Mary loves *to* improve her Time.

Of the Concord or Agreement of Words in a Sentence.

Q. WHAT does the Verb agree with?
A. The Verb agrees with it's Subject or Nominative Cafe, in Number and Perfon, as, *I love, thou loveft, we love, they love.*

Q. Has

Q. Has every Verb a Subject or Nominative Cafe ?

A. Yes; every Verb has a Subject or
Nominative Cafe, expreffed or implied.

Q. What, befide a fingle fubject, may
become the Subject or Nominative Cafe to
the Verb ?

A. A Noun fignifying more than one
thing may become the Nominative Cafe to
the Verb, and then the Verb may be put
either in the Singular or Plural number, as,
My *people is* foolifh, *they* have not known
me.

Q. Is there any thing elfe that may become the Subject of the Verb ?

A. Yes; the Infinitive Mode, or even a
claufe of a fentence, as, *To err* is human;
*To mourn for our Friends without Meafure,
is Folly.*

Q. What do Adjectives agree with ?

A. Adjectives, having no variation of
Gender or Number, cannot but agree in
thefe refpects with their Subftantives.

Q. Are

Q. Are there no Adjectives then that vary on account of number?

A. Yes; a few Pronominal Adjectives, which have the Plural Number, and agree in Number with their Subftantives, as, *This, that, enough; this man, thefe men, that boy, thofe boys, food enough, apples enow.*

Q. Do not fome Pronominal Adjectives agree with Nouns of the Singular Number only?

A. Yes; *Each, every, either,* agree with Nouns of the Singular Number only; as, *Each Man* in his Order; *Every* good *Man* fhall be happy; He loves *neither,* nor *either* cares for *him; Either* you or I are wrong.

Q. With what do Pronouns agree?

A. Pronouns muft agree with the Nouns they reprefent, or ftand for, in Number and Gender, as, George II. was King of Great-Britain, *he* was Grandfather to George III. Charlotte is Queen of Great-Britain, *fhe* was born in Germany.

Of the GOVERNMENT of
WORDS.

Q. IF a Pronoun comes before a Verb, in what Cafe fhall it be put ?

A. If a Pronoun comes before a Verb, it fhall be in the Nominative Cafe, as, *I* love, *we* hear.

Q. But if it follows the Verb ?

A. Then it fhall be in the Objective Cafe, as, He told *me*, I love *him*.

Q. Is there no exception to this rule?

A. The Verb *to be*, unlefs it is in the Infinitive Mode, is followed by the Nominative Cafe of the Pronoun, as, This is *he*, Who art *thou*, It is *I*.

Q. How may the Relation of Property or Poffeffion be expreffed ?

A. The Relation of Property or Poffeffion may be expreffed by the Poffeffive Cafe, as, The *King*'s Forces were victorious ; Teach me to feel *another*'s Woe.

Q. If

Q. If one Verb follows another, in what Mode fhall the latter be put?

A. If one Verb follows another, it fhall be put in the Infinitive Mode, with the Particle *to* before it, as, Boys love *to play.*

Q. Is not the Particle *to* fometimes omitted?

A. Yes; it is fometimes omitted after the Verbs, Bid, Dare, Make, Hear, See, and fome others.

Q. What Cafe follows the Participle Prefent?

A. The Participle Prefent governs the Objective Cafe of the Pronoun, as, We were feeking *him;* He was admonifhing *us.*

Q. What Cafe do Præpofitions govern?

A. Præpofitions govern the Objective Cafe of the Pronoun; as, He came with *me*; I ran from *him.*

Q. Have Adverbs and Interjections any government?

A. Adverbs

A. Adverbs and Interjections have no government.

Of the POSITION of WORDS.

Q. WHAT is the ufual place for the Nominative Cafe, denoting the Agent or Subject of Affirmation in an Affirmative Sentence?

A. The Nominative Cafe, denoting the Subject in an Affirmative Sentence, ufually goes before the Verb, as, The *Fire* burns.

Q. What is it's ufual place in an Interrogative Sentence?

A. In an Interrogative Sentence it either follows the Verb, or comes between the Auxiliary and the Verb, as, Loveft *thou?* or doft *thou* love?

A. What is it's place in an Imperative Sentence?

A. In an Imperative Sentence it ufually follows the Imperative Mode of the Verb; as, Go, *thou Trifler.*

Q. What

Q. What is the ufual place for the Objective Cafe, denoting the object of an
Affirmation?

A. It follows the Verb Active, as, Education forms the *Mind*. But if the Verb is
paffive, the Agent and Object change places,
as, The *Mind* is *formed* by Education.

Q. What is the ufual place of the Adjective?

A. Immediately before the Subftantive,
as, A *good* Man, a *fine* Houfe.

Q. But does it not fometimes follow the
Subftantive?

A. Yes; when a claufe of a fentence
depends upon the Adjective, the Adjective
is placed after the Subftantive, as, A *Man*
is *generous* to his Enemies.

Q. What is the moft convenient place
for an Adverb, or feparate claufe of a Sentence?

A. Between the Subject and the Verb;
as, Alexander *entirely* conquered Darius.
Alexander, *in three Battles*, conquered Darius.

3   Q. Is

Q. Is this a conſtant rule ?

A. No; Adverbs often precede the Adjectives, and follow the Verbs with which they are connected, as, Humility is not only a *very* excellent Virtue, but a *very* agreeable accompliſhment.

Q. Where is the uſual place of a Præpoſition?

A. A Præpoſition is uſually placed before the word to which it relates, as, He went *from* London *to* Hackney.

Q. But is it not ſometimes placed at the end of a ſentence?

A. Yes; as, Whom do you live *with*.

Q. Is not the common, order of words frequently changed?

A. Yes; eſpecially in poetry, in all ways in which it may be done without obſcurity or ambiguity.

Q. We have ſaid that Sentences may be divided into Simple and Compound: Of Simple Sentences you have ſpoken, but

what

what do you mean by a Compound Sentence?

A. Two or more Simple Sentences joined together by one or more connective words, become a Compounded Sentence, as, Blessed is the Man, *who* feareth the Lord, *and* keepeth his Commandments.

Q. How many sorts of Words are there, which connect Sentences?

A. Two; Relatives and Conjunctives.

Q. What do Relatives agree with?

A. The Relatives *Who, Which, That,* having no variation of Gender or Number, cannot but agree with their Antecedents.

Q. But do not some Relatives vary to express Gender, Number, and Person?

A. Yes; and these agree in Gender, Number, and Person, with their Antecedents.

Q. Must every Relative have an Antecedent to which it refers?

A. Yes; every Relative must have an Antecedent, either expressed or understood.

Q. Are

Q. Are the Relatives *Who* and *Which*, *What* and *That*, applied alike to things and perfons?

A. No; *Who* is applied to perfons only, and *Which*, to things; as, Blefſed is the Man *who* feareth always; Our Father, *who* art in Heaven; The Thing *which* you gave me; The Book *which* you lent me. The Pronoun *That* refers either to Perfons or Things, and *What* often includes the Antecedent and Relative.

Q. Is not the Relative fometimes the Nominative Cafe to the Verb?

A. Yes; when no other Nominative comes between it and the Verb; for otherwife the Relative is governed by fome Verb or Præpofition in it's own Member of the Sentence.

Q. In what Cafe fhall the Relative *Who* be put after the Conjunction *Than?*

A. The Relative *Who*, when it refers to no Verb or Præpofition underftood, muft, after the Conjunction *Than*, be put in the Objective Cafe, as, ——Than *whom*, Satan except, none higher fat.

F 2   N. B.

N. B. When *This* or *Thefe*, *That* or *Thofe*, refer to a preceding Sentence, *This* or *Thefe* refer to the latter, *That* or *Thofe* to the former member or claufe of it.

Q. What is the ufual place of the Relatives *Who*, *Which*, and *That*, in a Sentence?

A. The Relatives *Who*, *Which*, and *That*, follow their Antecedents, and ought clearly to point them out.

Q. Is not the Relative often omitted in a Sentence?

A. Yes; the Relative is often underftood or omitted, as, The Man I love, that is, The Man *whom* I love.

Q. What other fort of words, befide Relatives, did you fay connect Sentences?

A. Conjunctions.

Q. Have thefe any Government?

A. They have no Government of Cafes, but they have fometimes a Government of Modes; fome require the Indicative, fome the Subjunctive Mode after them; others have no influence at all on the Mode.

Q. Have

Q. Have not fome Conjunctions corre-
fpondent Conjunctions belonging to them ?

A. Yes ; fo that in the following member of the Sentence, the latter Conjunction
anfwers to the former ; as, for example,

In the following member of the Sentence,

Although requires *Yet*, or *Neverthelefs*.
Whether.......... *Or.*
Either.......... *Or.*
Neither........ *Nor.*
As............. *So*, implying comparifon.
As............. *As*, implying a comparifon
           of equality
So.............. *That*, expreffing a confe-
           quence

AN

APPENDIX,

CONTAINING

A CATALOGUE of VERBS

IRREGULARLY INFLECTED.

N. B. When the regular Form is alſo uſed, an Aſteriſm is put.

Preſent.	*Paſt.*	*Participle*
ABIDE.	Abode.	Abode.
Ariſe,	Aroſe.	Ariſen.
Awake.	Awoke.*	Awoke.*
Bear, *or bring forth.*	Bare.	Born.
Bear, *or carry.*	Bore,	Borne.
Beat.	Beat.	Beaten.
Begin.	Began.	Begun.
Bereave.	Bereft.*	Bereft.*
Beſeech.	Beſought.	Beſought.
Bid.	Bade.	Bidden.
		Bind.

Prefent	Paſt.	Participle.
Bind.	Bound.	Bound.
Bite.	Bit.	Bitten.
Blow.	Blew.	Blown.
Bleed.	Bled.	Bled.
Break.	Brake.	Broken, broke.
Breed.	Bred.	Bred.
Bring.	Brought.	Brought.
Burſt.	Burſt.	Burſt, burſten.
Buy.	Bought.	Bought.
Caſt.	Caſt.	Caſt.
Catch.	Caught.*	Caught.*
Chide.	Chid.	Chidden.
Chuſe.	Choſe.	Choſen.
Cleave.	Clave.	Cloven, cleft
Cling.	Clung.	Clung
Clothe.	Clad.*	Clad.*
Come.	Came.	Come.
Coſt.	Coſt.	Coſt
Creep.	Crept.	Crept.
Crow.	Crew.	Crowed.
Cut.	Cut.	Cut.
Dare.	Durſt.*	Dared.
Die.	Died.	Dead.
Dig.	Dug.*	Dug.*
Draw.	Drew.	Drawn

Drink.

Present.	Past.	Participle.
Drink.	Drank.	Drunk.
Drive.	Drove.	Driven
Eat.	Ate.	Eaten.
Fall.	Fell.	Fallen.
Feed.	Fed.	Fed.
Fight.	Fought.	Fought.
Find.	Found.	Found.
Flee, *from an Enemy.*	Fled.	Fled.
Fling.	Flung.	Flung.
Fly, *as a Bird.*	Flew,	Flown.
Forsake.	Forsook.	Forsaken.
Freeze.	Froze.	Frozen.
Get.	Gat, got.	Gotten.
Give.	Gave.	Given
Gnaw.	Gnawed.	Gnawn.
Go.	Went.	Gone.
Grind.	Ground.	Ground.
Grow.	Grew.	Grown.
Hang.	Hung.*	Hung, hanged.
Hew.	Hewed.	Hewn.
Hide.	Hid.	Hidden.
Hit.	Hit.	Hit
Hold.	Held.	Holden, held.
Hurt.	Hurt.	Hurt.

Keep.

Prefent.	*Paft.*	*Participle.*
Keep.	Kept.	Kept.
Knit.	Knitted.	Knitted, knit.
Know.	Knew.	Known.
Lay.	Laid.	Laid, lain.
Lead.	Led.	Led.
Leave.	Left.	Left.
Lend.	Lent.	Lent.
Lie.	Lay.	Lain.
Load.	Loaded.	Loaden, laden.
Lofe.	Loft.	Loft.
Make.	Made.	Made.
Meet.	Met.	Met.
Mow.	Mowed.	Mown.*
Pay.	Paid.	Paid.
Put.	Put	Put.
——	Quoth he.	——
Read.	Read.	Read.
Rend.	Rent.	Rent.
Ride.	Rode.	Ridden
Ring.	Rung, rang.	Rung.
Rive.	Rived.	Riven.
Rife,	Rofe.	Rifen.
Run.	Ran.	Run.
Saw.	Sawed.	Sawn.
Say.	Said.	Said.

See.

Present.	*Past.*	*Participle.*
See.	Saw.	Seen.
Seek.	Sought.	Sought.
Seethe.	Seethed.	Sodden.
Sell.	Sold.	Sold.
Send.	Sent.	Sent.
Set.	Set.	Set.
Shake.	Shook.	Shaken.
Shave.	Shaved.	Shaven.
Shear.	Sheared.	Shorn.
Shed.	Shed.	Shed.
Shine.	Shone.	Shone.
Shoe.	Shod.	Shod.
Shoot.	Shot.	Shot.
Show.⎤	Showed.	Shown.
Shew.⎦	Shewed.	Shewn.
Shrink.	Shrank, ſhrunk,	Shrunk.
Shut.	Shut.	Shut.
Sing.	Sang.	Sung.
Sink.	Sunk.	Sunk.
Sit.	Sate.	Sat.
Slay.	Slew.	Slain.
Slide.	Slided, ſlid.	Slidden.
Sleep.	Slept.	Slept.
Slink.	Slunk.	Slunk.
Sling.	Slung.	Slung.

Slit.

Present.	_Past._	_Participle_
Slit.	Slit.	Slit.
Smite.	Smote.	Smitten.
Sow.	Sowed.	Sown.
Speak.	Spoke.	Spoken.
Speed.	Sped.	Sped.
Spend.	Spent.	Spent.
Spin.	Spun.	Spun.
Spit.	Spat.	Spitten.
Split.	Split.	Split.
Spread.	Spread.	Spread.
Spring.	Sprung, sprang.	Sprung.
Stand.	Stood.	Stood.
Steal.	Stole.	Stolen.
Stick.	Stuck.	Stuck.
Sting.	Stung.	Stung.
Stink.	Stank.	Stunk.
Stride.	Strode, strid.	Stridden.
Strike.	Struck.	Stricken.
String.	Strung.	Strung.
Strive.	Strove.	Striven.
Strow.	Strowed.	Strown.
Swear.	Swore, sware.	Sworn.
Sweat.	Sweat.	Sweat.
Swell.	Swelled.	Swollen.
Swim.	Swam.	Swum.

3

Swing.

Present.	Past.	Participle.
Swing.	Swung.	Swung.
Take.	Took.	Taken.
Teach.	Taught.	Taught.
Tear.	Tore, tare.	Torn.
Tell.	Told.	Told.
Think.	Thought.	Thought.
Thrive.	Throve.	Thriven.
Throw.	Threw.	Thrown.
Thruſt.	Thruſt.	Thruſt.
Tread.	Trode.	Trodden.
Wax.	Waxed.	Waxen.
Wear.	Wore.	Worn.
Weave.	Wove.	Woven.
Weep.	Wept.	Wept.
Win.	Won.	Won.
Wind.	Wound.	Wound.
Work.	Wrought.	Wrought.
Wring.	Wrung.	Wrung.
Write.	Wrote.	Written.
Writhe.	Writhed.	Writhen.

F I N I S.

www.ingramcontent.com/pod-product-compliance
Lightning Source LLC
Chambersburg PA
CBHW021526090426
42739CB00007B/799